German
for Children
COURSE BOOK

Third Edition

Catherine Bruzzone

Illustrations by Clare Beaton

New York Chicago San Francisco Lisbon London Madrid Mexico City
Milan New Delhi San Juan Seoul Singapore Sydney Toronto

The McGraw·Hill Companies

Copyright © 2011, 2003, 1993 by The McGraw-Hill Companies, Inc. All rights reserved. Printed in China. Except as permitted under the United States Copyright Act of 1976, no part of this publication may be reproduced or distributed in any form or by any means, or stored in a database or retrieval system, without the prior written permission of the publisher.

6 7 8 9 10 11 12 13 14 15   DSS   21 20 19 18

ISBN   978-0-07-174503-1 (book and CD set)
MHID   0-07-174503-3 (book and CD set)

ISBN   978-0-07-174498-0 (book for set)
MHID   0-07-174498-3 (book for set)

Library of Congress Control Number: 2010925180

Also available
French for Children
Italian for Children
Spanish for Children
Each title in this series is a complete home learning course with CDs and a colorful children's Activity Book.

Produced for McGraw-Hill by
b small publishing

German edition
Claudia Eilers

Editor
Catherine Bruzzone

Design and Art Direction
Lone Morton

Typesetting
Lone Morton and Olivia Norton

Recordings
Gerald Ramshaw, Max II

Music
David Stoll

Lyrics
Claudia Eilers

Presenters
Claudia Eilers and Kenneth Price

Singers
Sean Klein and Margarete Forsyth

With special thanks to Claire Woolford-Fakoussa and her family, the children of Mossautal, Rosemary Cadigan, and Class 8a, Gymnasium Michelstadt, Odenwald, Germany.

McGraw-Hill books are available at special quantity discounts to use as premiums and sales promotions or for use in corporate training programs. To contact a representative, please e-mail us at bulksales@mcgraw-hill.com.

This book is printed on acid-free paper.

Contents

	Learning German	4
1	**Ich!**	5
	Saying hello; counting from 1 to 10; answering questions about yourself	
2	**Max und Marie**	11
	Saying "yes" and "no" if someone asks you if you like something	
3	**In der Schule**	17
	Saying where places are; talking with friends	
4	**Meine Familie**	23
	Introducing and talking about the family	
5	**Das Haus**	29
	Asking what something is; finding your way around the house	
6	**Unterwegs**	35
	Saying what you like and don't like to do; counting from 11 to 20	
7	**Rot und gelb**	41
	Describing things: colors; big and small; answering someone who is asking whether you want something	
8	**Der Zoo**	47
	Saying you feel hungry, thirsty, or afraid; saying you think something is good, large, funny, and so on; asking for things in a snack bar or restaurant	
9	**Das Picknick**	53
	Saying what the weather's like; saying "yes" or "no" if you're offered food	
10	**Herzlichen Glückwunsch!**	59
	Saying that you would like something or would like to do something	
	More about German	65
	Numbers 1 to 1000	68
	Songs	69
	Word List, German–English	74
	Word List, English–German	77

Learning German

Here are 10 simple suggestions to make learning German with Passport's *German for Children* much more fun:

 Learn with someone else if you can: perhaps a friend, your mom or dad, sister or brother. This course is full of games, so it's nice to have someone to play them with.

 Start with the cassette. Claudia will tell you what to do and when to use the book. Just remember to read Fun Facts and Super-Katze, and to fill in the checklist.

 Listen for a short while, then go and do something else. But don't give up! When you listen again, you'll be amazed how much you remember.

 Rewind and fast-forward the cassette, and go over any section as often as you like.

 Say everything out loud – don't keep it to yourself. You could practice while you're taking a bath or out on your bike.

 Don't worry if you make mistakes. That's just part of learning a language.

 Sometimes an English word can help you remember the German: "chocolate" and **Schokolade**, "house" and **Haus**, for example.

 Start a German scrapbook and put in everything you can discover about Germany – and the other countries where German is spoken, such as Austria and Switzerland.

 If you're learning with a friend, give each other German names. There are some suggestions for names below.

 Enjoy yourself! It's a lot of fun speaking another language . . . and one day it might be very useful too.

German names

Boys

Johannes	Kai
Sebastian	Stefan
Lorenz	Matthias
Oliver	Michael

Girls

Anke	Martina
Christine	Katrin
Katja	Sabine
Charlotte	Susanne

1 Ich!

This is Claudia.
You'll hear her voice
on the tape.
She's going to help you
learn German.

> Right from the start, you're going to learn:
>
> - to say "hello"
> - how to answer when someone asks you your name
> - the numbers from 1 to 10
> - how to answer when someone asks you how old you are.

Before you go on, listen to the tape.
Claudia will tell you what to do.
First, she's saying hello.
The words for the two songs you will hear are on page 69.

Naming names

Put an in the box when you hear the name.

☐	☐	☐	☐
Sebastian	**Sabine**	**Mark**	**Lisa**

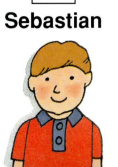

hallo
hello, hi

wie heißt du?
what's your name?

ich heiße _____
my name is

Fun Facts

Altogether more than 100 million people speak German as their first language. Can you find three countries, apart from Germany, where German is spoken? They are all in Europe.

In German, when you say hello to a grown-up, you should add **Frau** (Mrs) or **Herr** (Mr) to their name.

When you meet people, you shake hands to say hello to them. Practice saying hello, German-style!

Komm, zähl mit!

Listen to the tape.
Count these things with Claudia, and write the number in the box.

How old am I?

Listen to the tape. Match up the names with the ages. The first one has been done for you.

Draw a picture of yourself here. Why not add a speech bubble with **Guten Tag!** (good day!) or **Hallo!** (hi!)?

Ich! Me!

Ich heiße _____.

Ich bin ____ .

guten Tag!
good day!

wie geht's?
how are things?

danke, gut
fine, thanks

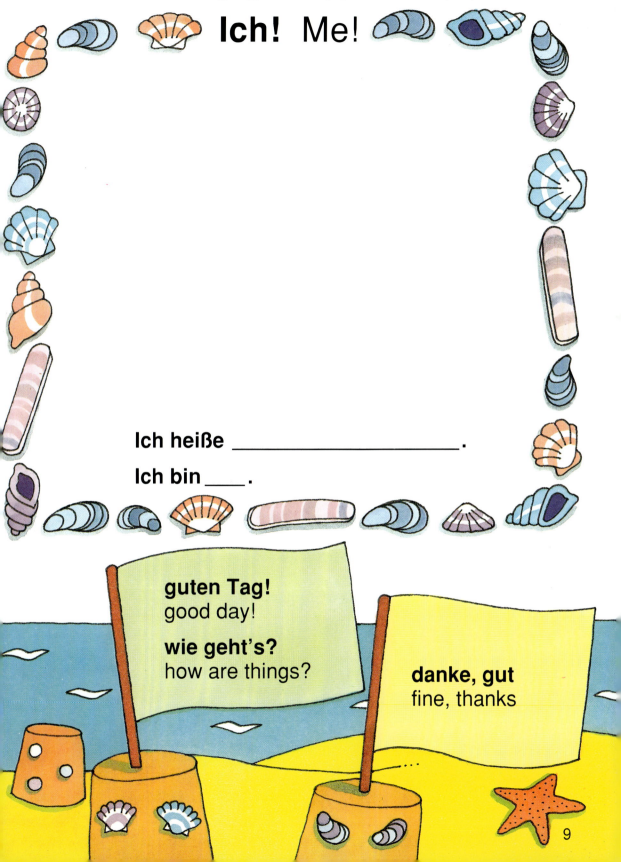

Checklist

Let's go over what you have learned in this unit. When you are sure you know what these mean, put a ✔ in the box.

☐ eins zwei drei vier fünf sechs sieben acht neun zehn

☐ guten Tag! hallo!

☐ ich heiße _____

☐ wie heißt du?

☐ ich bin _____

☐ wie alt bist du?

☐ wie geht's? danke, gut

Try and say these out loud. If you have any trouble with them, why not listen to the tape again?

Super-Katze!

Guten Tag, ich heiße Super-Katze.

Eins, zwei, drei, vier.

Hallo, ich heiße Monster-Ratte!

2 Max und Marie

In this unit, you're going to learn:

- to say whether you like something or not
- to say "yes" and "no," and
- the names of some popular – and unpopular – things!

What are they saying?

First listen to the tape.
Now cut out the sentences below and paste them into the right bubbles. Now can you fill in the blanks?

Ich bin _____	Ich heiße _____
Hallo	Ich bin _____	Guten Tag
	Ich heiße _____	

I like . . .

Listen to the tape. Draw a line between **Ja** and the things you like and **Nein** and the things you don't.

The words for the song are on page 69.

ich mag . . . I like . . .
magst du? do you like?
ja yes
nein no

Fun Facts

A good place to stop for a snack in Germany, is the **Imbiß,** or **Würstchenbude**. This is a stand where you can buy **Bratwurst**, grilled sausage, **Pommes frites**, french fries, and soft drinks, like **Apfelsaft**, apple juice.

Bratwurst

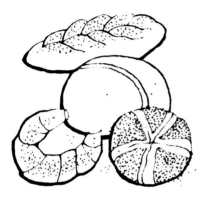

If you go to Germany, you must visit a **Bäckerei-Konditorei**, a bakery-pastry shop. They have an enormous variety of bread and rolls on display – some spiced with poppy seeds, onion, or caraway seeds; some rolled, knotted, or braided . . .

And look out for cakes like **Amerikaner**, **Apfelstrudel**, or **Bienenstich**, that means "bee sting." This is a cream-filled cake with an almond topping.

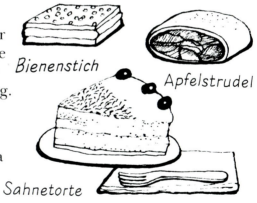
Bienenstich
Apfelstrudel
Sahnetorte

If the shop has a **Café**, treat yourself to a huge slice of **Sahnetorte**, cream cake, or a home-made **Eisbecher**, ice cream sundae.

Ja oder nein?

Listen to the tape.
Marie and Max's shopping trip.
If Marie or Max say they like something, check the box next to the right picture below. Then cut those pictures out and paste them in the basket on page 15.

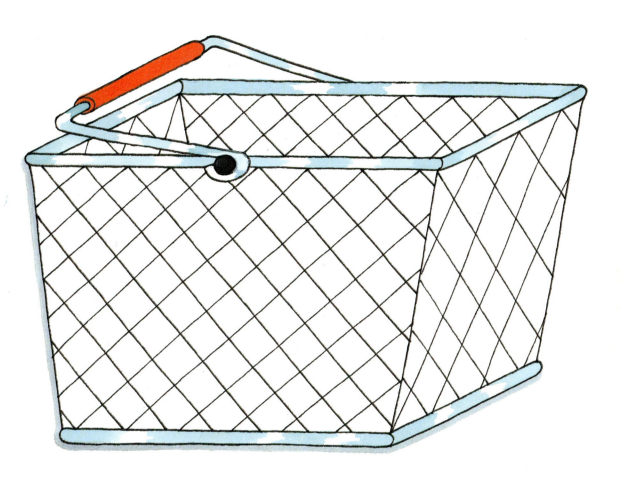

die Coca-Cola Coca-Cola
die Limonade lemonade
die Schokolade chocolate
die Katze cat
das Eis ice cream
die Erdbeere strawberry
die Pizza pizza
die Hexe witch
die Spinne spider
das Monster monster

Checklist

Let's go over what you have learned in this unit. When you are sure you know what these mean, put a ✓ in the box.

☐ **ich mag**

☐ **magst du?**

☐ **ja**

☐ **nein**

☐ **die Schokolade** **die Katze**
die Coca-Cola **die Spinne**
das Eis **das Monster**
die Limonade **die Erdbeere**
die Pizza **die Hexe**

Try and say these out loud. If you have any trouble with them, why not listen to the tape again?

Super-Katze!

Ich mag Schokolade, Eis und Limonade.

BANK

Ich mag Gold!

Igitt! Eine Spinne!

Bank = bank
Gold = gold

3 In der Schule

In this unit, you're going to learn:

- how to ask where something is
- how to say "goodbye" and "thank you"
- and some words about school.

Deal a number

This is a simple card game to practice the numbers from 1 to 10.
You need a deck of cards and a die – and a partner.
You need only the 1 to 10 of hearts and the 1 to 10 of spades.
The ace counts as 1. Shuffle the hearts and deal out five cards each.
Shuffle the spades and lay them around in a clock shape, face down.
Decide who goes first.

1 *Player 1*: you throw the die and call out the number in German.
2 Move around the clock face that number of cards, counting out loud in German as you go. Use the die as a counter.
3 When you land, turn over the card and say the number it shows, out loud in German.
4 If the number matches a card in your hand, pick it up and lay down the pair. If not, turn it face down again.
5 *Player 2*: now you throw the die, call out the number, and move on around the clock just like Player 1.
6 The first player with all the pairs wins.

Now listen to the tape. First you will hear a song about school. The words are at the back of the book on page 70.

17

Peter's first day

Listen to the tape and point to the places and things around the picture. As you point say, **"da"** (there).

die Schule the school

das Klassenzimmer

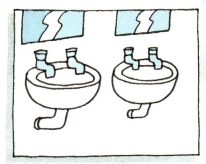

das Waschbecken

die Tür

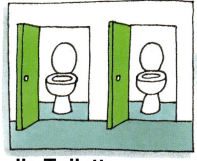

die Toilette

Fun Facts

German children start school at the age of six and they go to the **Grundschule**, elementary school, until they are ten.

To sweeten the first day at school, every **Schulanfänger**, new girl or boy, is given a huge cone, called a **Schultüte**, filled with candy, chocolate, and small surprises.

If German children don't get good grades on their report card, the **Zeugnis**, they have to repeat the year. This is called **sitzenbleiben**, that means "stay seated"!

School starts in the morning at about 8 o'clock, and finishes at lunchtime. German children have homework, but there is still lots of time left to play with friends in the afternoon.

They carry their school books in a backpack called a **Tornister** or **Schulranzen**.

Guess the card

Play this game with a friend.
Make 9 cards: trace or copy the pictures around the edge of the playground scene on pages 18 and 19. Shuffle them and lay them out face down.

1. *Player 1:* will ask where something is. Use, **"wo ist?"** or **"wo sind?"**
2. *Player 2:* points to a card and says, **"da."**
3. If the guess is right, *Player 2* wins a point.
4. The first player with 10 points wins. (Shuffle the cards between each try.)

Now go on to the activity on page 21 before you go back to the tape.

Hidden pictures

There are three things hidden in this picture.
Can you find them? These questions will give you a clue.

Wo ist die Schokolade?
Wo ist die Katze?
Wo sind die Freunde?

Then go back to the tape.

danke	thank you
auf Wiedersehen	goodbye
Tschüß	

Checklist

Let's go over what you have learned in this unit. When you are sure you know what these mean, put a ✓ in the box.

- [ ] wo ist?
- [ ] wo sind?
- [ ] da
- [ ] danke
- [ ] auf Wiedersehen   Tschüß
- [ ] die Schule   die Toilette
      die Lehrerin   der Schulhof
      die Freunde   das Klassenzimmer
      die Tür   das Waschbecken

Try and say these out loud. If you have any trouble with them, why not listen to the tape again?

4 Meine Familie

In this unit, you're going to learn:

- the names for "mom," "dad," "sister," and "brother"
- how you would be introduced to someone's family
- how to introduce your own family
- how to say how many brothers and sisters you have.

But first, listen to the tape and try the quiz. Then do the word puzzle below.

Puzzle

See if you can find these words hidden in the square. They're the same as the ones in the quiz, so you should know what they mean.

C	R	G	D	H	T	E	R	E	A
T	S	C	H	Ü	ß	H	T	O	G
A	L	R	V	L	E	T	A	R	U
K	N	S	D	A	N	K	E	D	T
L	E	O	K	L	D	T	S	R	E
E	I	N	T	O	V	S	E	T	N
V	Y	Z	W	E	I	S	A	H	R
N	G	E	L	A	E	U	N	C	T
E	D	H	E	L	R	F	A	J	A
E	I	N	S	U	N	E	S	T	G

EINS
VIER
TSCHÜB
ZWEI
JA
DANKE
GUTEN TAG
ZEHN

23

Familie Bumerang

Listen to the tape. You'll be meeting this kangaroo family.

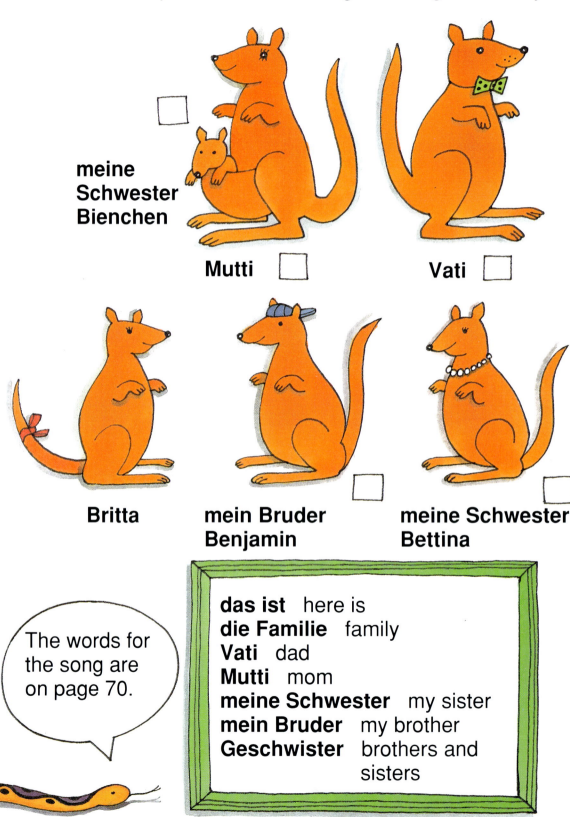

meine Schwester Bienchen

Mutti **Vati**

Britta **mein Bruder Benjamin** **meine Schwester Bettina**

The words for the song are on page 70.

das ist   here is
die Familie   family
Vati   dad
Mutti   mom
meine Schwester   my sister
mein Bruder   my brother
Geschwister   brothers and sisters

Fun Facts

Heiligabend, Christmas Eve, is the best family time in German-speaking countries. Children find their presents under the richly decorated Christmas tree, or **Tannenbaum**, that is lit by real candles.

For the special Christmas lunch, **Weihnachtsgans**, roast goose with red cabbage, is served.

Four weeks before Christmas, for Advent, families bake **Stollen**, fruit cake, **Plätzchen**, cookies, and **Lebkuchen**, ginger bread.

Do you know how to wish someone Merry Christmas in German?
Frohe Weihnachten!

ich habe ___ Brüder	I've got ___ brothers
ich habe ___ Schwestern	I've got ___ sisters
ich habe keine Brüder	I don't have any brothers
ich habe keine Schwestern	I don't have any sisters
ich habe keine Geschwister	I don't have any brothers or sisters

Meine Familie

Draw a picture of your own family.
Copy the labels below, so you can describe your picture in German. Then try the game on page 27.

| meine Schwester | mein Bruder | Mutti | Vati |

| ich habe ___ Schwestern | ich habe ___ Brüder |

| ich habe keine Brüder | ich habe keine Schwestern |

| ich habe keine Geschwister |

You may also need:
my grandma, **meine Oma**, and my grandpa, **mein Opa**.

Das ist meine Familie

This is an "introducing game" for 2 players.
You need a die and two markers (buttons will do fine).
Decide who goes first.

1. *Player 1:* throw the die and move that number of spaces – count in German as you go!
2. When you land, introduce the person who appears on that square to *Player 2*. Say, **"das ist . . ."**
3. *Player 2:* you reply, **"guten Tag,"** and then it's your turn to throw the die.
4. The first player to reach the ice cream wins.

 Mutti

 Vati

meine Schwester

mein Bruder

Checklist

Let's go over what you have learned in this unit. When you are sure you know what these mean, put a ✓ in the box.

- [ ] **das ist**
- [ ] **Mutti   Vati**
- [ ] **meine Schwester**
      mein Bruder
- [ ] **ich habe _____ Brüder**
- [ ] **ich habe _____ Schwestern**
- [ ] **ich habe keine Brüder**
      ich habe keine Schwestern
      ich habe keine Geschwister

Try and say these out loud. If you have any trouble with them, why not listen to the tape again?

Super-Katze!

Familie Monster-Ratte.

Da ist Vati!

Ich habe fünf Säcke Gold.

Säcke = sacks

Danke, Vati!

5 Das Haus

In this unit, you're going to learn:

- another answer to the question "where is?" **(wo ist?)**
- how to ask "what's that?" – very useful if you don't know the name of something in German!
- and how to give the answer
- to understand the word for "please"
- the names for rooms and furniture in the home.

Start with this game.
Listen to the tape before you read ahead.

Which hand?

You've probably played this game before. Now play it in German!
You'll need a partner. You're going to guess which
hand your partner's holding something in.
Find a pebble, a **Kieselstein.**

1 Now one of you will hold the pebble
   behind your back and ask your partner:
   "Wo ist der Kieselstein?"
2 Your partner must touch one of your
   arms and say **"da"** (there).
3 If it's right, he or she wins one point.
4 Then change places.
5 The first to get 10 points wins.

29

Was ist das?

You'll need a partner to play this game.
First cut out some small pieces of paper, this size:
and cover the pictures in the maze below.

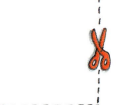

1 *Player 1:* call out a number from 1 to 6 in German.
2 *Player 2:* start from that number and find the way to the picture.
3 Uncover it and ask, **"was ist das?"**
4 *Player 1*: Give the answer, **"das ist ein . . ."** or **"das ist eine . . ."**
5 Then it's *Player 2's* turn to call a number.

You could make new picture cards like these with some of the other words you know and play the game again.

eine Katze **eine Tür** **ein Eis** **eine Coca-Cola**

Fun Facts

In Southern Germany, Austria, and Switzerland, where there is a lot of snow in winter, older houses have double windows to keep out the cold: one set opens outward, the other inward. They also have wooden shutters, **Fensterläden**, and deep overhanging roofs for the snow to slide off.

In summer, the windows of German houses have plant boxes full of brightly colored flowers. The outsides of some houses are also decorated with pictures and old-style German writing, called Gothic.

𝕲𝖆𝖘𝖙𝖍𝖔𝖋

Beds usually have large, square feather pillows and big, cosy comforters called **Federbetten**.

Listen to the song on tape. You can join in with the words, which are on page 71 at the back of the book.

Checklist

Let's go over what you have learned in this unit. When you are sure you know what these mean, put a ✓ in the box.

☐ **was ist das?**

☐ **das ist ein/eine . . .**

☐ **hier**

☐ **bitte**

☐ **das Haus**   **ein Tisch**
    die Küche   **ein Kühlschrank**
    das Badezimmer   **ein Stuhl**
    das Wohnzimmer   **ein Fernseher**
    das Schlafzimmer   **ein Bett**

Try and say these out loud. If you have any trouble with them, why not listen to the tape again?

6 Unterwegs

In this unit, you're going to learn:

- to say what you like doing
- to say what you don't like doing
- to count up to 20.

Spot the differences

First, there are 5 differences between these two pictures. Can you spot them? The answers are under Picture 1. Next, can you name 8 things in Picture 1, out loud in German?
You'll hear the answers on tape.

Label on bottle; picture; cakes on plate; dials on TV; pattern on tablecloth.

Im Auto

Listen to the tape.
What does the Berger family like to do in the car?

was machst du gern? what do you like to do?
ich lese gern I like to read
ich höre gern Radio I like to listen to the radio
ich esse gern I like to eat
ich singe gern I like to sing
ich esse nicht gern I don't like to eat
ich singe nicht gern I don't like to sing

Speeding and traffic jams

This is a game like *Chutes and Ladders* – you speed up the empty freeways and crawl back down into the traffic jams! You'll need a partner, two markers (buttons will do), and a die.
The first to get to the country in the last square wins.
If you land on any of these pictures, you must say, in German:

Can you guess what these two are saying?

37

Spin a number

You can play this game on your own or with a friend.
Make the spinner from a piece of cardboard. Trace or copy the shape shown here. Push a pencil or stick through the center. Twirl the spinner and say the number that it rests on, out loud in German. Take turns if you are playing with a friend.

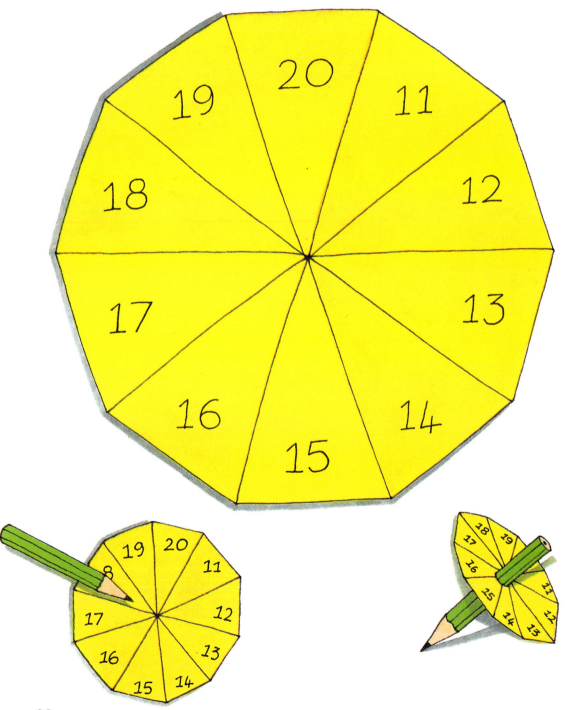

Fun Facts

In Germany, you can tell where a car comes from by its license plate. Big cities have one letter, **B** for **Berlin**, **M** for **München** (Munich). Smaller towns have two letters, and country areas, **Landkreise**, have three. If you want to know the name of the area, it's written on a small round stamp on the license plate.

In many German, Austrian, and Swiss cities, there are train tracks in the streets. They are for electric streetcars, **Straßenbahn** or **Tram**. Compared with cars and buses, streetcars make no noise, and they don't pollute the air.

Bingo

Use a pencil to fill in this card with any numbers from 1 to 20. (If you don't press too hard, you can erase them and play again.) Then listen to the tape and cross out the numbers as they are called. Can you get your parents or a friend to play with you and call out different numbers?

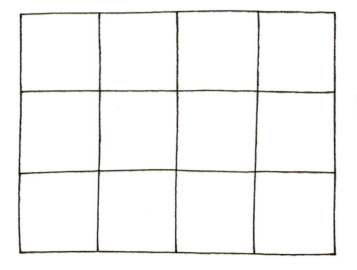

Checklist

Let's go over what you have learned in this unit. When you are sure you know what these mean, put a ✓ in the box.

☐ elf   zwölf   dreizehn   vierzehn   fünfzehn
  sechzehn   siebzehn   achtzehn   neunzehn   zwanzig

☐ was machst du gern?

☐ ich singe gern
  ich esse gern
  ich höre gern Radio

☐ ich reise nicht gern
  ich lese nicht gern
  ich schlafe nicht gern

Try and say these out loud. If you have any trouble with them, why not listen to the tape again?

7 Rot und gelb

In this unit, you're going to learn:

- the colors
- how to say "big" and "small"
- and to understand someone who is asking you what you want.

Listen to the tape before you go on. There's a song to start off with. The words are on page 72.

Welche Farbe?

Point to the colors as you hear them on tape.

Racing colors

Who will reach the finish line first?
You can play with one or two partners – or even on your own.
Cut out the horses below, and decide who starts. You need a die.

1. *Player 1*: throw the die and move that number of squares along the track – counting in German, of course.
2. Each time, say the color of the square you land on in German.
3. If you can't remember it, or if it's wrong, go back two squares.
4. Then it's *Player 2's* turn to throw the die.

Match the colors

First make 10 cards to match the squares on the boards below, the same size and color. They can be paper or cardboard. Then put them in a box or mix them up on the floor, face down.
You'll need a partner to play this game.
Choose a board and decide who starts.

1 *Player 1:* will pick a card from the box and call out the color in German.
2 Whoever has that color on their board calls out, **"für mich!"** (for me!).
3 They then take the card and place it on their board on the matching square.
4 Then it's *Player 2's* turn to pick a card.
5 The first to cover a board is the winner.

für mich! for me!

Take your pick

Listen to the tape. Decide which balloon is being called and mark the correct box.

Fun Facts

Here are three flags of countries where German is spoken. Can you find out what colors they should be and color them in yourself?

Deutschland **Österreich** **Schweiz**

45

Checklist

Let's go over what you have learned in this unit. When you are sure you know what these mean, put a ✓ in the box.

☐ **blau rot schwarz weiß gelb
grau grün lila braun orange**

☐ **groß**

☐ **klein**

☐ **möchtest du . . . ?**

☐ **bitte schön**

☐ **für mich**

Try and say these out loud. If you have any trouble with them, why not listen to the tape again?

8 Der Zoo

In this unit, you're going to learn:

- the names of some zoo animals
- how to say you're hungry, thirsty, or afraid
- how to ask for something in a snack bar or restaurant
- how to say that something's super, big, great, etc.

Listen to the tape before you go on.

Die Tiere

Here are the animals you'll be meeting in this unit. Can you spot 5 differences between the two pictures?

Do the activity on page 48 before you go back to the tape.

Giraffe: leaves; dolphin/mouth; elephant/tusks; monkey/tail; lion/ears.

47

Where are they?

Fit each animal below into its place in the picture above.

_____ _____ _____ _____ _____

Can you write in the names of these animals in German?
Look back at page 47, if you need help.
Then go back to the tape.

Are they hungry or thirsty?

Listen to the tape.
These animals will say if they are hungry or thirsty.
Draw some food or a drink for them in the box next to each animal. If you're not sure what they eat, just make it up.

was ist los? what's the matter?
ich habe Hunger I'm hungry
ich habe Durst I'm thirsty
ich habe Angst I'm scared
ich auch me too

Snick snack

Listen to the children ordering a snack at the zoo snack bar. Draw a line to connect the food and drink each child orders. The first one has been done for you.

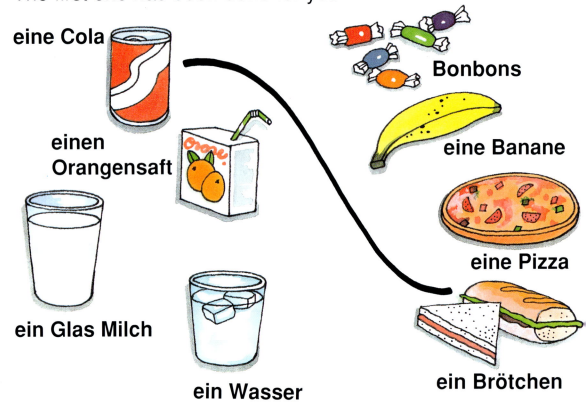

Now trace or copy those pictures and play a game with a friend. One person be the snack bar owner and the other ask for a drink and a snack. Try to use all the language in the hamburger below. You could also use pictures of other things you already know in German: ice cream, strawberries, lemonade, and so on.

(ein Brötchen), bitte
  (a sandwich), please
das da, bitte that, please
ist das alles? is that all?
wieviel kostet das? how much is that?
(zwanzig) Mark (twenty) marks*

*German numbers from 1 to 1000 are on page 68.

Fun Facts

Everything stops in Germany for **Karneval**, Carnival, also called **Fastnacht**. The cities of **Köln**, Cologne, and **Mainz** have famous street parades with huge floats. Bunches of candy are thrown into the crowd. People go in fancy dress and sing and dance in the streets. In Bavaria and Austria, Carnival is called **Fasching**.

In the town of **Basel**, in Switzerland, people wear strange wooden masks as a **Fastnacht** disguise. This is a tradition that goes right back to the Middle Ages.

das ist groß! it's big!
das ist super! it's super!
das ist witzig! it's fun!
das ist toll! it's great!
das ist lecker! it's good! (of food)

The words for the song are at the back of the book on page 72.

Checklist

Let's go over what you have learned in this unit. When you are sure you know what these mean, put a ✓ in the box.

☐ **was ist los?**

☐ **ich habe Hunger**   **ich habe Durst**   **ich habe Angst**

☐ **der Löwe**   **der Delphin**   **der Affe**
   der Elefant   **die Giraffe**

☐ **eine Banane**   **einen Orangensaft**
   ein Glas Milch   **Bonbons**
   ein Wasser   **ein Brötchen**

☐ **das ist groß!**   **das ist toll!**   **das ist lecker!**
   das ist witzig!   **das ist super!**

☐ **das da, bitte**   **wieviel kostet das?**   **ist das alles?**

9 Das Picknick

> In this unit, you're going to learn:
> - how to talk about the weather
> - how to answer if someone offers you "a little" food
> - the names of some food in German.

First let's listen to the weather song on tape. The words are on page 73.

What's the weather like today?

Listen to the tape and write an ✗ next to the right picture.

es ist heiß it's hot
es ist kalt it's cold

es ist schönes Wetter the weather's fine
es regnet it's raining

53

Fun Facts

The regions of Germany all have delicious food to offer. Can you guess where the **Frankfurter** comes from?

A great favorite with children is **Kartoffelsalat** und **Würstchen**, potato salad and hot dogs.
A **Berliner** is a jelly doughnut. Do you know where that name comes from? A hamburger, although it sounds like the German city, Hamburg, is an American idea. In Germany, it's called **Frikadelle** and it doesn't come on a bun!

In the South, **Sauerkraut**, pickled white cabbage, with heaps of smoked pork and steaming dumplings, **Knödel**, keeps you warm on a winter's day.

If you like cheese, Switzerland's the place to go. After a hard day's skiing, try some **Raclette**, melted cheese served with pickles and potatoes, or **Käse-Fondue**, cubes of bread dipped into a bowl of bubbling melted cheese. That will revive you!

Go to Austria if you have a sweet tooth! Try **Kaiserschmarren**, stips of pancake with raisins and almonds, **Marillenknödel**, apricot dumplings, and the famous **Sachertorte**, a rich, dark chocolate cake with apricot jam filling.

Yum, yum

Find the picture that matches the first one in each row.
Check the tape to hear how you say these foods in German.

das Brot

der Käse

der Salat

Äpfel

Tomaten

Kuchen

In der Sonne

Listen to the conversation on tape.
Here is the picture it's describing.
Can you match the sentences below with the people in the picture who are saying them?
Write the sentences in the speech bubbles, if you want.

Checklist

Let's go over what you have learned in this unit. When you are sure you know what these mean, put a ✓ in the box.

- [ ] **es ist schönes Wetter**
- [ ] **es ist kalt**
- [ ] **es ist heiß**
- [ ] **es regnet**
- [ ] **möchtest du etwas . . . ?**
- [ ] **das Brot**   **der Salat**
      der Käse   **die Tomate**
      der Apfel   **der Kuchen**
- [ ] **guten Appetit!**   **danke**

Try and say these out loud. If you have any trouble with them, why not listen to the tape again?

Super-Katze!

O nein, es regnet!

Es ist aus!

Es ist kalt.

es ist aus = it's finished, it's over

10 Herzlichen Glückwunsch!

In this unit, you're going to learn:
- how to say that you'd like something
- how to say the names of some popular toys
- and you'll go over some of the language you've learned before.

Before you start, listen to the tape. The words for the song are on page 73.

Memory game

Can you remember the names of these things in German?
Say them out loud.
Now listen to the tape again.
Moritz and Marion would like these for their birthday.

Geschenke

Birthday presents. Fit these jigsaw pieces together, and you'll find out what the other children on tape would like for their birthday.

ich möchte gern . . . I'd like . . .
was möchtest du? what do you want?
viele lots of
der Geburtstag birthday

Pairs game

Make 24 simple cards – two for each of these pictures.

 eine Katze ein Radio
 einen Hund Bücher
 Bonbons Filzstifte
 ein Fahrrad ein Springseil
 ein Auto eine Puppe
 einen Luftballon  viele Geschenke

You'll need a partner.
Deal out the cards – 12 each.
The aim is to collect pairs, so lay down any pairs you have at the start.

1 *Player 1:* ask for a card to join to one of yours to make a pair. For example, if you have one dog, ask for another.
   Say, **"ich möchte gern eine Katze."**
2 Then it's *Player 2's* turn to do the same.
3 The first to lay down all the cards wins.

Fun Facts

Obstkorb (fruit basket) is a fun German party game. All the players sit in a circle, on chairs, cushions, or sheets of paper. They choose a fruit: **Apfel**, apple, **Birne**, pear, **Pflaume**, plum, or **Banane**, banana.

One player stands in the middle and calls out two fruits, like **"Apfel und Birne!"** While those fruits trade places, the player in the middle tries to snatch a seat. Whoever loses the seat, keeps calling. If the caller shouts **"Der Obstkorb fält um!"**, the fruit basket falls over, then things get really wild, because everyone has to change places!

Party quiz game

It's more fun to play this game with a partner, but you can play on your own too.
You'll need a die and markers.

1. Take turns throwing the die and move your marker along the board.
2. The first to reach the cake wins – but on the way, you must follow the instructions, out loud in German!
3. You miss a turn if you can't answer.

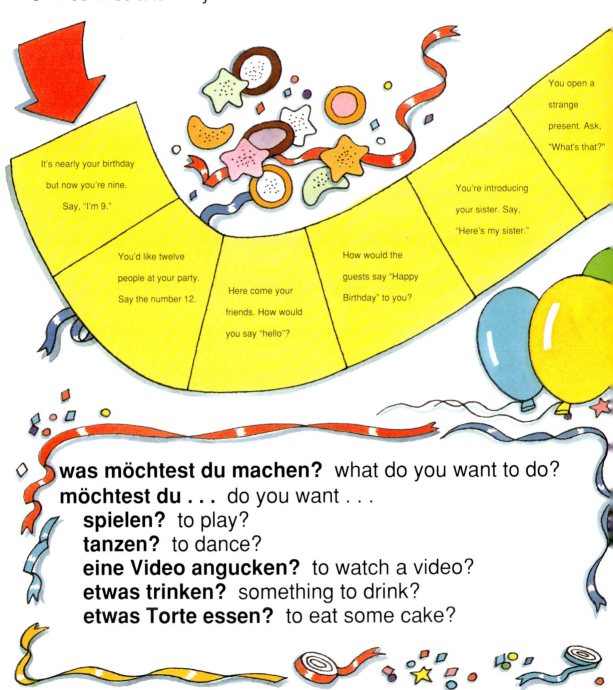

It's nearly your birthday but now you're nine. Say, "I'm 9."

You'd like twelve people at your party. Say the number 12.

Here come your friends. How would you say "hello"?

How would the guests say "Happy Birthday" to you?

You're introducing your sister. Say, "Here's my sister."

You open a strange present. Ask, "What's that?"

◊ **was möchtest du machen?** what do you want to do?
möchtest du . . . do you want . . .
   spielen? to play?
   tanzen? to dance?
   eine Video angucken? to watch a video?
   etwas trinken? something to drink?
   etwas Torte essen? to eat some cake?

Checklist

Let's go over what you have learned in this unit. When you are sure you know what these mean, put a ✓ in the box.

☐ **was möchtest du?**

☐ **ich möchte gern . . .**

☐ **einen Hund   eine Puppe**
   ein Fahrrad   eine Torte   ein Springseil
   Bücher   Filzstifte   viele Geschenke

☐ **was möchtest du machen?**

☐ **möchtest du . . .**
   tanzen?   eine Video angucken?
   spielen?   etwas trinken?

☐ **Herzlichen Glückwunsch!**

More about German

Learning a language is like breaking a code or recognizing patterns. Did you notice some patterns in the German you have just learned? Have a look at these:

The words for "the"

There are three words for "the" in German:

- **der, die,** and **das**

der Apfel   the apple
die Katze   the cat
das Haus   the house

- When you have more than one thing, you just use **die**:

die Äpfel   the apples
die Katzen   the cats
die Häuser   the houses

The words for "a"

There are two words for "a" in German:

- **ein** and **eine**

ein Apfel   an apple
eine Katze   a cat
ein Haus   a house

Can you spot the pattern?
If you use **der** or **das** for "the," you use **ein** for "a."
And if you use **die** for "the," you use **eine** for "a."

The **der/ein** words are called *masculine*.
The **die/eine** words are called *feminine*.
The **das/ein** words are called *neuter*.
All *nouns* (objects, people, and places) in German are masculine, feminine, or neuter.

As you would expect, the words for "man" and "boy" are masculine, and the word for "woman" is feminine.

Look at these examples:

ein Mann	a man	**eine Frau**	a woman
ein Vater	a father	**eine Mutter**	a mother
ein Onkel	an uncle	**eine Tante**	an aunt
ein Lehrer	a man teacher	**eine Lehrerin**	a woman teacher
ein Junge	a boy		

But, the words for "girl" and "child" are neuter: **ein Mädchen** (girl) and **ein Kind** (child).

So for most nouns, there's no easy way of telling whether you should use **der**, **die**, or **das** or **ein** or **eine** – you just have to learn each word! Don't panic, after a while you can hear if you've got it right . . . and people will still understand you, even if you get it wrong.

Sometimes you will also hear **einen**, **einem**, or **einer**, and **den** and **dem**. In Unit 9, you learned to ask for **einen orangensaft**, and in Unit 10 you learned **ich möchte gern einen Hund** and **ich möchte gern einen Luftballon**. If you go on learning German, you will find out more about this, but don't worry about it now.

Have you noticed that when they are written, German nouns always start with a capital letter? Look back through your book to check this.

More than one thing

Look at this pattern:

Tomate	tomato	**Erdbeere**	strawberry
Tomaten	tomatoes	**Erdbeeren**	strawberries
Katze	cat		
Katzen	cats		

In German, just as in English, the noun usually changes when it is *plural* (when you have more than one of it). So in the examples above, you add an -**n**, **Tomaten**, **Katzen**, and **Erdbeeren**.

Many of the nouns you met in this book add an -**n** in the plural. But not all German nouns do. The best thing is to try to memorize the plurals as you meet them. For example, do you remember these?

Apfel apple
Äpfel apples

Geschenk present
Geschenke presents

Try and say all those words out loud. If you can't remember how to pronounce them, listen to your cassettes again.

As you get better at German, keep trying to break the code and discover more patterns. Soon you'll be able to make up your own sentences. (There are lots of patterns to discover in the numbers on the next page!)

Numbers 1 to 1000

1	eins	60	sechzig
2	zwei	61	einundsechzig
3	drei	62	zweiundsechzig

and the same again to . . . 69

4	vier	70	siebzig
5	fünf	71	einundsiebzig
6	sechs	72	zweiundsiebzig
7	sieben		
8	acht		
9	neun		
10	zehn		

and on to . . . 79

11	elf	80	achtzig
12	zwölf	81	einundachtzig
13	dreizehn	82	zweiundachtzig

and still the same pattern to . . . 89

14	vierzehn	90	neunzig
15	fünfzehn	91	einundneunzig
16	sechzehn	92	zweiundneunzig
17	siebzehn		
18	achtzehn		
19	neunzehn		
20	zwanzig		

and on to . . . 99, and then

21	einundzwanzig	100	hundert
22	zweiundzwanzig	101	hunderteins
23	dreiundzwanzig	102	hundertzwei
24	vierundzwanzig	103	hundertdrei

and the same pattern as from 1 to 100 up to . . . 199

25	fünfundzwanzig	200	zweihundert
26	sechsundzwanzig	300	dreihundert
27	siebenundzwanzig	400	vierhundert
28	achtundzwanzig	500	fünfhundert
29	neunundzwanzig	600	sechshundert
30	dreißig	700	siebenhundert
31	einunddreißig	800	achthundert
32	zweiunddreißig	900	neunhundert
		1000	tausend

with the same pattern as 20 . . . to 39

40	vierzig
41	einundvierzig
42	zweiundvierzig

and on with the same pattern to . . . 49

50	fünfzig
51	einundfünfzig
52	zweiundfünfzig

and then the same pattern to . . . 59

Songs

Unit 1

Song 1
Ich heiße Moritz, hallo.
Wie heißt du?
Wie heißt du?
Ich heiße Moritz, hallo.
Wie heißt du?
Wie heißt du?

Ich heiße Moritz
Wie geht's?
Ich heiße Moritz
Wie geht's?

Gut,
Sehr gut.

Ich heiße Susi, hallo.
Wie heißt du?
Wie heißt du?
Ich heiße Susi, hallo.
Wie heißt du?
Wie heißt du?

Ich heiße Susi.
Wie geht's?
Ich heiße Susi.
Wie geht's?

Gut,
Sehr gut.

Song 2
Eins, zwei, drei,
Vier, fünf, sechs,
Sieben, acht, neun,
Zehn.

Eins, zwei, drei,
Vier, fünf, sechs,
Sieben, acht, neun,
Zehn.

Unit 2

Magst du Coca-Cola?
Nein, nein, nein.
Magst du Limonade?
Nein, nein, nein.
Magst du Erdbeeren und Eis?
Nein, nein, nein.

Magst du Pizza?
Ja!
Nichts als Pizza?
Ja!

Magst du Coca-Cola?
Nein, nein, nein.
Magst du Limonade?
Nein, nein, nein.
Magst du Erdbeeren und Eis?
Nein, nein, nein.

Magst du Pizza?
Ja!
Nichts als Pizza?
Ja!

nichts als = nothing but

Eins, zwei, drei, vier,
Fünf, sechs, sieben,
acht, neun, zehn.

Unit 3

**Gehst du gern zur Schule?
Ja, es geht.
Gehst du gern zur Schule?
Ja, es geht.**

**Wo ist der Lehrer?
Da ist der Lehrer.
Wo sind die Freunde?
Da sind die Freunde.**

**Gehst du gern zur Schule?
Ja, es geht.**

gehst du gern? = do you like going?
zur = to (the)

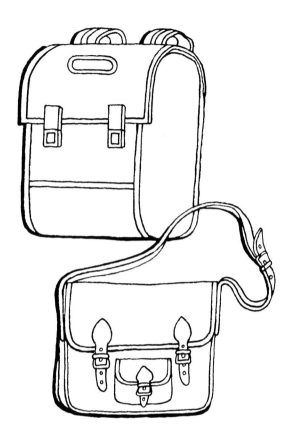

Unit 4

**Das ist meine Familie.
Das ist meine Familie.**

**Das ist Mutti.
Das ist Vati.
Das ist Oma.
Das ist Opa.
Ich hab' sieben Schwestern.
Und ich hab' sechs Brüder.**

**Das ist meine Familie.
Das ist meine Familie**

Unit 5

Was ist das?
Was ist das?
Das ist eine Hexe.
Was ist das?
Was ist das?
Das ist eine Hexe.

Wo ist die Hexe?
Sie ist hier,
Hier in der Küche.
Ja, in der Küche.

Wo ist sie jetzt?
Jetzt ist sie hier.
Hier im Wohnzimmer?
Ja, im Wohnzimmer.

Was ist das?
Was ist das?
Das ist eine Hexe.

Was ist das?
Was ist das?
Das ist eine Hexe.

sie = she
jetzt = now

Unit 6

Ich esse nicht gern.
Ich lese nicht gern.
Ich reise nicht gern.
Was mache ich gern?
Schlafen!

Ich esse nicht gern.
Ich lese nicht gern.
Ich reise nicht gern.
Was mache ich gern?
Schlafen!

Ich höre nicht gern Radio.
Ich fahre nicht gern Auto
Was mache ich gern? . . .
Oh . . .
Schlafen!

was mache ich gern? =
what do I like to do?

Unit 7

Gelb, rot, blau!
Luftballons.
Schwarz, weiß, grau!
Luftballons.

Gelb, rot, blau!
Luftballons.
Schwarz, weiß, grau!
Luftballons.

Möchtest du den kleinen?
Möchtest du den großen?
Möchtest du den gelben?
Möchtest du den roten?

Möchtest du den kleinen?
Möchtest du den großen?
Möchtest du den gelben?
Möchtest du den roten?

Gelb, rot, blau!
Luftballons.
Schwarz, weiß, grau!
Luftballons.

Gelb, rot, blau!
Luftballons.
Schwarz, weiß, grau!
Luftballons.

Gelb, rot, blau!
Luftballons . . .

den kleinen = the little one
den großen = the big one
den gelben = the yellow one
den roten = the red one

Unit 8

Wir gehen in den Zoo.
Da gibt's viele Tiere.
Wir gehen in den Zoo.
Da gibt's viele Tiere.

Wir gehen in den Zoo.
Da gibt's viele Tiere.
Wir gehen in den Zoo.
Da gibt's viele Tiere.

Es gibt Löwen, es gibt Affen,
Elefanten und Giraffen.

Wir gehen in den Zoo.
Da gibt's viele Tiere.
Wir gehen in den Zoo.
Da gibt's viele Tiere.

Das ist super! Das ist toll!
Tschüß.
Das ist super! Das ist toll!
Tschüß.

wir gehen = we're going
gibt's
es gibt } = there are
viele = lots of

Unit 9

Es ist schönes Wetter.
Es ist heiß.
Heute gibt's ein Picknick,
Ein Picknick und ein Eis.
Lecker, lecker, lecker,
Toll!

Es ist schönes Wetter.
Es ist heiß.
Heute gibt's ein Picknick,
Ein Picknick und ein Eis.
Lecker, lecker, lecker,
Toll!

Nein, oh nein!
Jetzt regnet es.
Es ist kalt,
Sehr kalt.

Ah!

Es ist schönes Wetter.
Es ist heiß.
Heute gibt's ein Picknick,
Ein Picknick und ein Eis.
Lecker, lecker, lecker,
Toll!

heute = today
gibt's = there is
sehr = very

Unit 10

Du hast heute Geburtstag.
Du hast heute Geburtstag.
Eins, zwei, drei, vier,
Fünf, sechs, sieben.
Möchtest du tanzen?
Möchtest du singen?

Du hast heute Geburtstag.
Du hast heute Geburtstag.
Eins, zwei, drei, vier,
Fünf, sechs, sieben.
Möchtest du essen?
Möchtest du trinken?

Herzlichen Glückwunsch!
Sieben, acht, neun, zehn.
Herzlichen Glückwunsch!
Hier ist ein Geschenk . . .
Geschenk.

Du hast heute Geburtstag.
Du hast heute Geburtstag.
Eins, zwei, drei, vier,
Fünf, sechs, sieben.
Möchtest du lesen?
Möchtest du spielen?
Du hast heute Geburtstag.
Du hast heute Geburtstag.

Tschüß!

heute = today

Word list

All the German nouns are listed with **der**, **die** or **das**.

German–English

A
aber but
acht eight
achtzehn eighteen
der Affe monkey
alles all;
  ist das alles? is that all?
alt old
Angst fear;
  ich habe Angst I'm scared
angucken to watch
der Apfel apple
auch also, as well, too
auf: auf Wiedersehen goodbye
aus: es ist aus it's finished, it's over
das Auto car;
  Auto fahren to drive;
  im Auto in the car

B
das Badezimmer bathroom
die Banane banana
die Bank bank
die Bäckerei bakery
das Bett bed
(Ich) bin I am
bis bald! see you soon!
(du) bist you are
bitte please
bitte schön here you are
blau blue
der Bonbon candy
braun brown
das Brot bread
das Brötchen bread roll, sandwich
der Bruder brother
das Buch book;
  die Bücher books

C
die Coca-Cola Coca-Cola;
  die Cola Coke

D
da there;
  da, bitte schön! there you are!
danke thank you;
  danke, gut fine, thanks
das that;
  das ist here is, that is
dein, deine your
der Delphin dolphin
Deutschland Germany
dich you, yourself
dick fat
der Dieb thief
drei three
dreizehn thirteen
du you
Durst: ich habe Durst I'm thirsty

E
ein, eine a
eins one
das Eis ice cream
der Elefant elephant
elf eleven
er he
die Erdbeere strawberry
es it;
  es ist it is
essen to eat
etwas some

F
das Fahrrad bike
die Farbe color
die Familie family
der Fernseher TV, television;
  fernsehen to watch TV
fertig? ready?
der Filzstift felt-tip pen
Frau Mrs., madam, ma'am
die Frau wife, woman

die Freunde friends
fünf five
fünfzehn fifteen
für for;
  für mich for me
  für dich for you

G

der Geburtstag birthday
gehen to go;
  gehst du gern? do you like to go?;
  wie geht's? how are things?
gelb yellow
das Geschenk present
die Geschwister brothers and sisters
gibt's, es gibt there is, there are
die Giraffe giraffe
das Glas glass;
  ein Glas a glass of
das Gold gold
grau gray
groß big, tall
die Grundschule elementary school
grün green
gut fine, good
guten Appetit! enjoy your meal!
guten Tag good day

H

haben to have;
  ich habe I have;
  du hast you have
hallo! hi! hello!
halt! stop!
das Haus house
heiß hot;
  es ist heiß *(weather)* it's hot
heiße: ich heiße my name is;
  wie heißt du? what's your name?
Herr Mr.
herzlichen Glückwunsch zum Geburtstag! happy birthday!
heute today
die Hexe witch
hier here;
  hier ist here is
der Hund dog
Hunger: ich habe Hunger I'm hungry

I

ich I, me;
  ich auch me too
in in, at
der Inspektor inspector
ist is;
  es ist it is

J

ja yes
das Jahr year
der Jahrmarkt amusement park
jetzt now
der Junge boy

K

kalt cold;
  es ist kalt *(weather)* it's cold
die Katze cat
der Käse cheese
kein, keine no, not
der Kieselstein pebble
das Kind child
das Klassenzimmer classroom
klein little, small
komm come (on)
der Kuchen *(small)* cake
die Küche kitchen
der Kühlschrank fridge, refrigerator

L

der Lehrer *(man)* teacher;
die Lehrerin *(woman)* teacher
lecker *(food)* good
lesen to read
lila purple
die Limonade soda pop, lemonade
los geht's! lets go! off you go!
der Löwe lion
der Luftballon balloon

M

machen to do, to make;
  ich mache I do
  du machst you do

(ich) mag I like;
  magst du? do you like?
der Mann man
die Mark mark *(German money)*
das Mädchen girl
mein, meine my
mich me
die Milch milk
das Monster monster
möchte want;
  ich möchte I want;
  ich möchte gern I'd like;
  möchtest du? do you want?
die Mutter mother
Mutti mom

N
nach after
nein no
neun nine
neunzehn nineteen
nicht not
nichts als nothing but
noch einmal one more time, once more
nur only

O
oder or
die Oma grandma
der Onkel uncle
der Opa grandpa
orange *(color)* orange

der Orangensaft orange juice
Österreich Austria

P
das Papier paper
das Picknick picnic
die Pizza pizza
die Pommes frites french fries
prima! well done!; great!
die Puppe doll

R
das Radio radio
die Ratte rat
(es) regnet (it is) raining
die Reise trip
reisen to travel
rot red

S
der Sack bag
der Salat salad, lettuce
schlafen to sleep
das Schlafzimmer bedroom
die Schokolade chocolate
schön beautiful;
  bitte schön here you are;
  schönes Wetter fine weather
die Schule school;
  in der Schule at school
der Schulhof playground

schwarz black
die Schweiz Switzerland
die Schwester sister
sechs six
sechzehn sixteen
sehr very
sie she
sieben seven
siebzehn seventeen
sind are;
  das sind these are
singen to sing
die Sonne sun;
  in der Sonne in the sun
spielen to play
die Spinne spider
das Springseil jump rope
der Stuhl chair
super super

T
der Tag day
die Tante aunt
tanzen to dance
das Tier animal
der Tisch table
die Tochter daughter
die Toilette public bathroom
toll! great!
die Tomate tomato
die Torte cake
trinken to drink
Tschüß goodbye, 'bye
die Tür door

U
und and
unterwegs on a trip

V
der Vater father
Vati dad
die Videokassette videocassette
viele, viel lots of, a lot;
 viel Spaß! have fun!
vier four
vierzehn fourteen

W
was? what?;
 was ist das? what's that?
 was ist los? what's the matter?
 was machst du gern? what do you like to do?
 was möchtest du machen? what do you want to do?
das Waschbecken sink
das Wasser water
weiß white
welche? which?
das Wetter weather
wie alt bist du? how old are you?
wie geht's? how are things?
wie heißt du? what's your name?
wieviel kostet das? how much is that

wir we
witzig fun
wo? where?;
 wo ist? where is?;
 wo sind? where are?
das Wohnzimmer living room

Z
zählen to count;
 zähl mit! let's count!
zehn ten
der Zoo zoo
zu to;
 zur Schule to school
zuhören to listen;
 hör zu! listen!
zwanzig twenty
zwei two
zwölf twelve

English–German

A
a ein, eine
after nach
all alles;
 is that all? ist das alles?
also auch
am bin
amusement park der Jahrmarkt
and und
animal das Tier
(you) are du bist
apple der Apfel
(they) are sie sind;
 these are das sind
as well auch
at in, auf
aunt die Tante
Austria Österreich

B
bag der Sack
bakery die Bäckerei
balloon der Luftballon
banana die Banane
bank die Bank
bathroom das Badezimmer; *(public)* die Toilette
bed das Bett
bedroom das Schlafzimmer
big groß
bike das Fahrrad
birthday der Geburtstag

77

black schwarz
blue blau
book das Buch
boy der Junge
bread das Brot
brother der Bruder
brown braun
but aber

C

cake die Torte; *(small)* der Kuchen
candy der Bonbon
car das Auto;
  in the car im Auto;
  to drive Auto fahren
cat die Katze
chair der Stuhl
cheese der Käse
child das Kind
chocolate die Schokolade
classroom das Klassenzimmer
Coca-Cola die Coca-Cola;
  Coke die Cola
cold kalt
color die Farbe
to count zählen;
  let's count! zähl mit!

D

dad Vati
to dance tanzen
daughter die Tochter
day der Tag
to do machen
dog der Hund

doll die Puppe
dolphin der Delphin
door die Tür
to drink trinken

E

to eat essen
eight acht
eighteen achtzehn
elementary school die Grundschule
elephant der Elefant
eleven elf
enjoy your meal! guten Appetit!

F

family die Familie
fat dick
father der Vater
felt-tip pen der Filzstift
fifteen fünfzehn
fine *(weather)* schön;
  fine thanks danke, gut
finished aus;
  it's finished es ist aus
five fünf
for für;
  for me für mich;
  for you für dich
four vier
fourteen vierzehn
french fries die Pommes frites
fridge der Kühlschrank
friends die Freunde
fun witzig,
  have fun! viel Spaß!

G

Germany Deutschland
giraffe die Giraffe
girl das Mädchen
glass das Glas;
  a glass of ein Glas
to go gehen;
  do you like to go? gehst du gern?
gold das Gold
good gut; *(food)* lecker
goodbye auf Wiedersehen, Tschüß
good day guten Tag!
grandma die Oma
grandpa der Opa
gray grau
great! toll!
green grün

H

happy birthday! herzlichen Glückwunsch zum Geburtstag!
to have haben;
  I have ich habe;
  you have du hast
he er
hello! hallo!
hi! hallo!
here hier;
  here is das ist, hier ist;
  here you are bitte schön
hot heiß
house das Haus
how are things? wie geht's?

how many? wieviele?
how old are you? wie alt bist du?
hungry: I'm hungry ich habe Hunger

I
I ich
ice cream das Eis
in in
inspector der Inspektor
is ist;
  it is es ist, das ist
it es

J
jump rope das Springseil

K
kitchen die Küche

L
lemonade die Limonade
let's go! los geht's!
lettuce der Salat
(I) like ich mag
(do you) like? magst du?
(I'd) like ich möchte gern
lion der Löwe
to listen zuhören;
  listen! hör zu!
living room das Wohnzimmer
lots, a lot viele, viel

M
ma'am, madam Frau
man der Mann
mark die Mark
me ich, mich;
  for me für mich;
  me too ich auch
milk die Milch
mom Mutti
monkey der Affe
monster das Monster
mother die Mutter
Mr. Herr
Mrs. Frau
my mein, meine;
  my name is ich heiße

N
name: my name is ich heiße;
  what's your name? wie heißt du?
nine neun
nineteen neunzehn
no nein; kein, keine
not nicht
now jetzt

O
off you go! los geht's!
one ein/eine;
  one more time, once more noch einmal
only nur
or oder
orange *(color)* orange
orange juice der Orangensaft

P
paper das Papier
pebble der Kieselstein
picnic das Picknick
pizza die Pizza
to play spielen
playground der Schulhof
please bitte
present das Geschenk
purple lila

R
radio das Radio
(it is) raining (es) regnet
rat die Ratte
to read lesen
ready? fertig?
red rot
refrigerator der Kühlschrank
repeat after me! sprich mir nach!

S
salad der Salat
sandwich *(roll)* das Brötchen
scared: I'm scared ich habe Angst
school die Schule;
  at school in der Schule;
  to school zur Schule
see you soon! bis bald!
seven sieben
seventeen siebzehn
she sie

to sing singen
sink das Waschbecken
sir Herr
sister die Schwester
six sechs
sixteen sechzehn
to sleep schlafen
small klein
soda pop die Limonade
some etwas
soon bald
spider die Spinne
stop! halt!
strawberry die Erdbeere
sun die Sonne;
  in the sun in der Sonne
super! super!
Switzerland die Schweiz

T

table der Tisch
tall groß
teacher *(man)* der Lehrer, *(woman)* die Lehrerin
television, TV der Fernseher;
  to watch television fernsehen
ten zehn
thank you danke
that das
there da;
  there is, there are gibt's, es gibt
there you are! da, bitte schön!

thief der Dieb
thirsty: I'm thirsty ich habe Durst
thirteen dreizehn
three drei
to zu
today heute
tomato die Tomate
too auch;
  me too ich auch
to travel reisen
trip die Reise;
  on a trip unterwegs
twelve zwölf
twenty zwanzig
two zwei

U

uncle der Onkel

V

very sehr
videocassette die Videokassette

W

(I) want ich möchte;
  do you want? möchtest du?
to watch angucken
water das Wasser
we wir
weather das Wetter
well done! Prima!

what? was?;
  what do you like to do? was machst du gern?;
  what do you want to do? was möchtest du machen?;
  what's that? was ist das?;
  what's the matter? was ist los?;
  what's your name wie heißt du
where? wo?;
  where is? wo ist?;
  where are? wo sind?
which? welche
white weiß
wife die Frau
witch die Hexe
woman die Frau

Y

year das Jahr
yellow gelb
yes ja
you du, dich;
  for you für dich
your dein, deine

Z

zoo der Zoo